SHORT WALKS
MADE EASY

NORFOLK COAST AND BROADS

Ordnance Survey

Contents

Getting outside on the Norfolk Coast and Broads	6
We smile more when we're outside	8
Respecting the countryside	10
Using this guide	11
Walk 1 King's Lynn	**14**
Walk 2 Old Hunstanton	**20**
Photos Scenes from the walks	26
Walk 3 Wells-next-the-Sea	**28**
Walk 4 Blakeney	**34**
Photos Wildlife interest	40
Walk 5 Sheringham to West Runton	**42**
Walk 6 Buxton	**48**
Walk 7 Toad Hole	**54**
Photos Cafés and pubs	60
Walk 8 Potter Heigham	**62**
Walk 9 Winterton-on-Sea	**68**
Walk 10 Burgh Castle	**74**
Credits	80

Map symbols	Front cover flap
Accessibility and what to take	Back cover flap
Walk locations	Inside front cover
Your next adventure?	Inside back cover

2 Short Walks Made Easy

Walk 1
KING'S LYNN

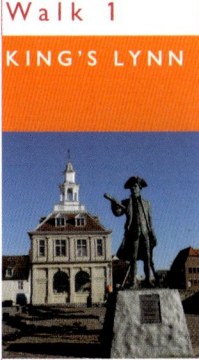

Distance
2.8 miles / 4.6km

Time
1½ hours

Start/Finish
King's Lynn

Parking PE30 5DY
Boal Quay car park, Hardings Way

Cafés/pubs
King's Lynn

Old port and town stroll with easy-going riverside path and ferry ride

Page 14

Walk 2

OLD HUNSTANTON

Distance
3.4 miles / 5.5 km

Time
2 hours

Start/Finish
Old Hunstanton

Parking PE36 6EL
Clifftop car park

Cafés/pubs
Old Town Beach Café;
The Mariner Inn

Coastal dunes and long sandy beach follow a walk by the River Hun

Page 20

Walk 3

WELLS-NEXT-THE-SEA

Distance
3.9 miles / 6.25 km

Time
2¼ hours

Start
Wells-next-the-Sea

Finish Bus stop, Holkham

Parking NR23 1AS
RCP car park, Freeman Street

Cafés/pubs
Wells-next-the-Sea Beach Café; The Lookout

England's largest NNR; pinewoods; salt marsh; Holkham Beach and Hall

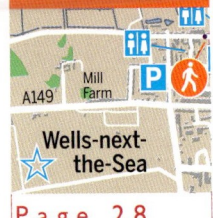

Page 28

Walk 4

BLAKENEY

Distance
2.3 miles / 3.7 km

Time
1½ hours

Start/Finish
Blakeney

Parking NR25 7NF
The Quay

Cafés/pubs
Blakeney

Boats along The Quay; views from Friary Hills; embankment-top walk

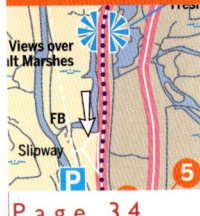

Page 34

Walk 5

SHERINGHAM TO WEST RUNTON

Distance
2.7 miles/4.25km

Time
1½ hours *STEAM TRAIN CATCH A BUS*

Start Sheringham station
Finish West Runton station

Parking NR26 8RG
Station Approach car park

Cafés/pubs
Sheringham, West Runton and West Runton beach

A linear clifftop walk on the Norfolk Coast Path; train ride back to start

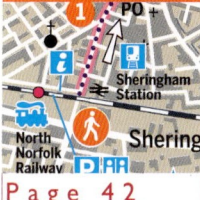

Page 42

Walk 6

BUXTON

Distance
2.8 miles/4.5km

Time
1¾ hours *STEAM TRAIN CATCH A BUS*

Start/Finish
Buxton

Parking NR10 5ET
Bure Valley Walk car park

Cafés/pubs
The Black Lion, Buxton

Peaceful Bure Valley Walk; tourist railway; Oxnead Hall; old church

Page 48

Walk 7

TOAD HOLE

Distance
3.75 miles/6km

Time
2¼ hours *CATCH A BUS*

Start/Finish
Ludham

Parking NR29 5QA
Lay-by, Norwich Road, opposite King's Arms

Cafés/pubs
King's Arms, Ludham

River Ant, electric boat trip, Toad Hole Cottage and How Hill Gardens

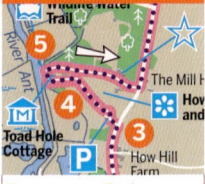

Page 54

4 Short Walks Made Easy

Walk 8
POTTER HEIGHAM

Distance
4.1 miles/6.6km

Time
2½ hours

Start/Finish
Potter Heigham

Parking NR29 5LL
St Nicholas's Church
(not on grass bank)

Cafés/pubs
Falgate Inn, Potter Heigham

Woodland and reed beds; Hickling Broad; medieval church

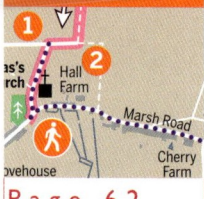

Page 62

Walk 9
WINTERTON-ON-SEA

Distance
3.4 miles/5.4km

Time
2 hours *CATCH A BUS*

Start/Finish
Winterton-on-Sea

Parking NR29 4AJ
Winterton Beach car park

Cafés/pubs
Dunes Café; Poppy's Tea Room; Fishermans Return

Sandy beach; Winterton Dunes NNR; ghostly church ruin; farmland

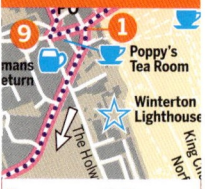

Page 68

Walk 10
BURGH CASTLE

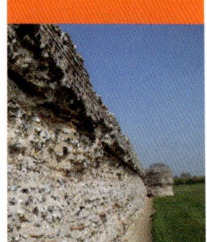

Distance
2.5 miles/4km

Time
1½ hours *CATCH A BUS*

Start/Finish
Burgh Castle: at the Queen's Head bus stop or the castle car park

Parking NR31 9QG
Burgh Castle car park

Cafés/pubs
Queen's Head, Burgh Castle

Roman fortress ruins; extensive reed beds and Breydon Water views

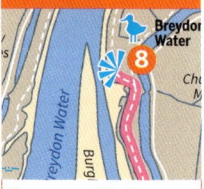

Page 74

Contents 5

GETTING OUTSIDE ON THE NORFOLK COAST AND BROADS

> " the walk at Winterton encounters a ghostly church and a wide sandy beach used by grey seals to pup in late autumn

OS Champion
Tom Wake

Winterton-on-Sea

A very warm welcome to the new Short Walks Made Easy guide to the Norfolk Coast and Broads – what a fantastic selection of leisurely walks we have for you here!

Featuring walks in the Broads National Park, from Aylsham to Burgh Castle, and the Norfolk Coast National Landscape, from The Wash to Winterton-on-Sea, this guide visits some of Norfolk's most outstandingly beautiful places.

In the Broads National Park, Britain's smallest by area at 117 square miles, you can relax and enjoy the tranquility of the Bure Valley at Buxton, and take to an electric boat wildlife trail from How Hill. From Potter Heigham, the route follows a path through wetland woodland and reed beds fringing Hickling Broad, while at Burgh Castle you can enjoy the views at Breydon Water, a haven for overwintering birds, before admiring the significant Roman fortress ruins. Combining the best of the Broads and Coast, the walk at Winterton encounters a ghostly church and a wide sandy beach used by grey seals to pup in late autumn.

Routes use sections of the Norfolk Coast Path, leading you through the dunes at Old Hunstanton and exploring the pine woods and extensive beach at Holkham. From the old harbour of Blakeney, you rise to the Friary Hills for far-reaching coastal marsh views before taking an embankment-top stroll across them, while from the 206-foot-high Beeston Bump you can relish the clifftop views between Sheringham and West Runton.

Tom Wake, OS Champion

WE SMILE MORE
WHEN WE'RE OUTSIDE

River Thurne close to Potter Heigham

Whether it's a short walk during our lunch break or a full day's outdoor adventure, we know that a good dose of fresh air is just the tonic we all need.

At Ordnance Survey (OS), we're passionate about helping more people to get outside more often. It sits at the heart of everything we do, and through our products and services, we aim to help you lead an active outdoor lifestyle, so that you can live longer, stay younger and enjoy life more.

We firmly believe the outdoors is for everyone, and we want to help you find the very best Great Britain has to offer. We are blessed with an island that is beautiful and unique, with a rich and varied landscape. There are coastal paths to meander along, woodlands to explore, countryside to roam, and cities to uncover. Our trusted source of inspirational content is bursting with ideas for places to go, things to do and easy beginner's guides on how to get started.

It can be daunting when you're new to something, so we want to bring you the know-how from the people who live and breathe the outdoors. To help guide us, our team of awe-inspiring OS Champions share their favourite places to visit, hints and tips for outdoor adventures, as well as tried and tested accessible, family- and wheelchair-friendly routes. We hope that you will feel inspired to spend more time outside and reap the physical and mental health benefits that the outdoors has to offer. With our handy guides, paper and digital mapping, and exciting new apps, we can be with you every step of the way.

To find out more visit os.uk/getoutside

RESPECTING
THE COUNTRYSIDE

You can't beat getting outside in the British countryside, but it's vital that we leave no trace when we're enjoying the great outdoors.

Let's make sure that generations to come can enjoy the countryside just as we do.

 Leave no trace

 Keep dogs under control; bin and bag waste

 Do not light fires; only BBQ at official sites

 Leave gates as you find them

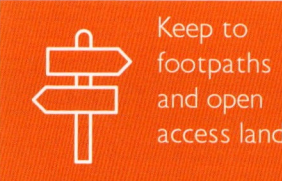 Keep to footpaths and open access land

 Plan ahead for your trip

For more details please visit gov.uk/countryside-code

USING THIS GUIDE

Easy-to-follow Norfolk Coast and Broads walks for all

Before setting off

Check the walk information panel to plan your outing

- Consider using **Public transport** where flagged. If driving, note the satnav postcode for the car park under **Parking**
- The suggested **Time** is based on a gentle pace
- Note the availability of **Cafés**, tearooms and pubs, and **Toilets**

Terrain and hilliness

- **Terrain** indicates the nature of the route surface
- Any rises and falls are noted under **Hilliness**

Walking with your dog?

- This panel states where **Dogs** must be on a lead and how many stiles there are – in case you need to lift your dog
- Keep dogs on leads where there are livestock and between April and August in forest and on grassland where there are ground-nesting birds

A perfectly pocket-sized walking guide

- Handily sized for ease of use on each walk
- When not being read, it fits nicely into a pocket...
- ...so between points, put this book in the pocket of your coat, trousers or day sack and enjoy your stroll in glorious countryside – we've made it pocket-sized for a reason!

Flexibility of route presentation to suit all readers

- **Not comfortable map reading?** Then use the simple-to-follow route profile and accompanying route description and pictures
- **Happy to map read?** New-look walk mapping makes it easier for you to focus on the route and the points of interest along it
- **Read the insightful Did you know?, Local legend, Stories behind the walk** and **Nature notes** to help you make the most of your day out and to enjoy all that each walk has to offer

OS information about the walk

- Many of the features and symbols shown are taken from Ordnance Survey's celebrated **Explorer** mapping, designed to help people across Great Britain enjoy leisure time spent outside

- National Grid reference for the start point
- Explorer sheet map covering the route

OS information
🚶 TF 617195
Explorer 236

The easy-to-use walk map

- **Large-scale** mapping for ultra-clear route finding

- **Numbered points** at key turns along the route that tie in with the route instructions and respective points marked on the profile

- **Pictorial symbols** for intuitive map reading, see Map Symbols on the front cover flap

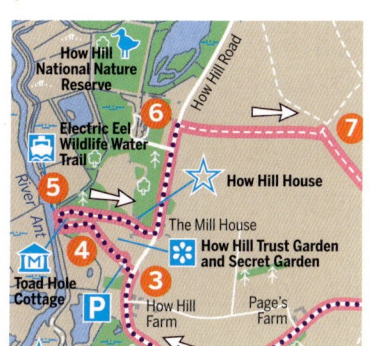

The simple-to-follow walk profile

- Progress easily along the route using the illustrative profile, it has **numbered points** for key turning points and **graduated distance** markers

- Easy-read **route directions** with turn-by-turn detail

- Reassuring **route photographs** for each numbered point

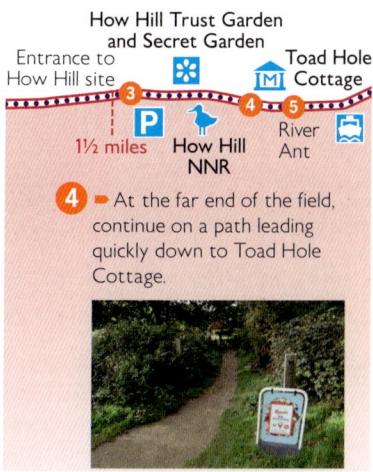

4 ▶ At the far end of the field, continue on a path leading quickly down to Toad Hole Cottage.

12   Short Walks Made Easy

Using QR codes

- Scan each QR code to see the route in Ordnance Survey's OS Maps App.
NB You may need to download a scanning app if you have an older phone

- OS Maps will open the route automatically if you have it installed. If not, the route will open in the web version of OS Maps

- Please click **Start Route** button to begin navigating or **Download Route** to store the route for offline use

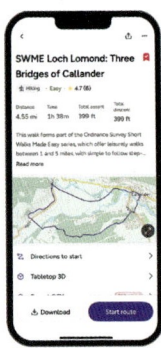

Norfolk Coast and Broads

WALK 1

KING'S LYNN

It may surprise visitors to the little coastal market town of King's Lynn that in the 14th century it was the most important port in England. Founded on the River Great Ouse in Saxon times, it grew to prominence as part of the Hanseatic League. This walk explores both sides of the river, taking in the historic dockside area. It also includes a ride on the King's Lynn Ferry (bit.ly/LynnFerry), which has been in operation since at least 1285.

OS information
TF 617195
Explorer 236

Distance
2.8 miles/4.6km

Time
1½ hours

Start/Finish
King's Lynn

Parking PE30 5DY
Boal Quay car park, Hardings Way

Public toilets
Western ferry terminus ④, Ferry Street, between ⑤ and ⑥, bus station

Cafés/pubs
King's Lynn

Terrain
Pavement and cobbles; asphalt, concrete and grassy paths; raised walkway to the ferry at ④

Hilliness
Level throughout; steps to/from the ferry at ④ and ⑤

Footwear
Year round

Public transport
King's Lynn has a railway station and a bus station, with frequent services: nationalrail.co.uk; traveline.info

Local legend King's Lynn is home to so many ghosts it's a wonder any of the townsfolk get any sleep. True's Yard Fisherfolk Museum (see p16) is said to be the town's most haunted building, claiming at least 37 resident phantoms. These include murky figures seen gazing out of the cottages' windows and a poltergeist known as Henry. The Duke's Head and Tudor Rose hotels are among other supernatural hotspots.

Did you know? The name King's Lynn is an upgrade from the town's former moniker, Bishop's Lynn. The latter was an anglicisation of Len Episcopi, a name given because the port came under the authority of the Bishop (*episcopus* in Latin) of Norwich. That all changed in 1537 with the Dissolution of the Monasteries, when Henry VIII took control and it became Lenne Regis (*regis* meaning 'of the king'). However, locals refer to the place simply as Lynn.

Accessibility

The ferry crossing between ④ and ⑤ is not accessible for wheelchairs, but otherwise this walk is wheelchair and pushchair friendly

Dogs
Welcome but keep on leads. No stiles

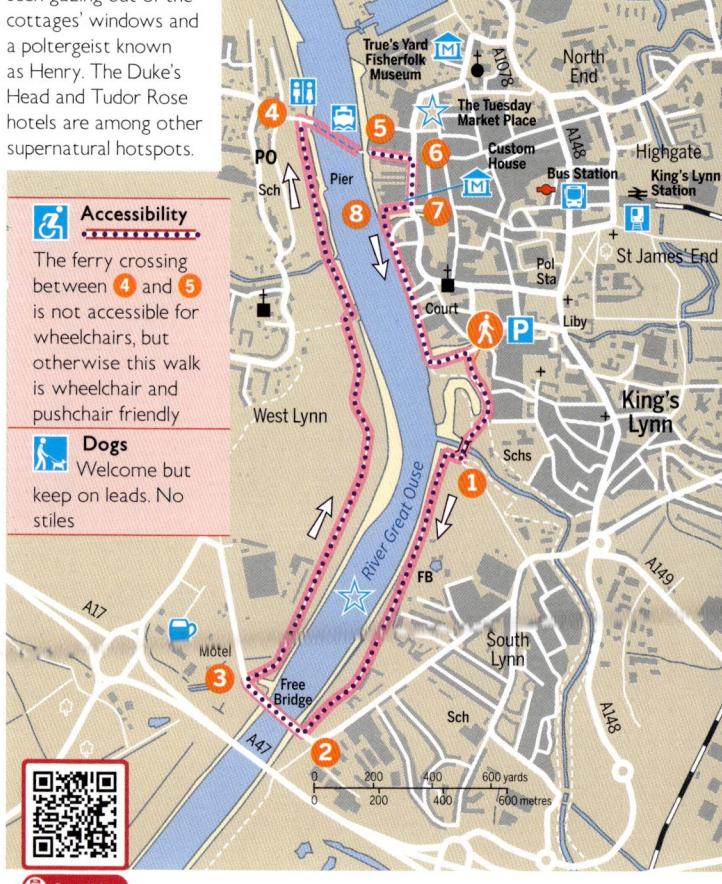

Walk 1 King's Lynn

STORIES BEHIND THE WALK

🏛 True's Yard Fisherfolk Museum

A commemoration of the days when fishing formed a major part of King's Lynn's economy, this museum incorporates the town's last surviving fisherfolk yard, cottages and smokehouse. Built in the late 18th century, the cottages housed fishing families and today give a rare and fascinating insight into working-class lives in the Georgian era. Also on display are models showing King's Lynn in Tudor and late Victorian times (truesyard.co.uk).

☆ The Tuesday Market Place

The area where King's Lynn's weekly market takes place (yes, on a Tuesday) has seen some grisly goings-on. In the late Middle Ages, women deemed to have practised witchcraft were burnt at the stake here. On the wall of one 16th-century building (number 15/16), you'll see an engraving marking the spot where the heart of one alleged witch, Margaret Read, supposedly landed when it burst from her body during execution.

Boal Quay car park

➡ From Boal Quay short-term car park turn **right** along Hardings Way.
➡ Continue on the tarmac path to a cyclepath/footpath signpost in ¼ mile, just after crossing a bridge.

Hardings Way — East bank, River Great Ouse — ½ mile

1 ➡ Turn **right** to walk on the path alongside the River Great Ouse to a bridge spanning the river in ⅔ mile.

16 Short Walks Made Easy

☆ River Great Ouse

As its name suggests, this is the longest of the four rivers in England called 'Ouse', rising 75 miles away in Northamptonshire. The 'Ouse' in this case is probably derived from the Celtic word for water. The section of the Great Ouse that this walk explores came into being in the 13th century when the river moved eastward from its old course during extensive flooding.

☆ Hanseatic League

The port at what is now King's Lynn began to develop not long after the river's shift to the east. But what really made the town was the emergence of the Hanseatic League. This was a confederation of market towns and merchant guilds that was founded in Germany and spread across Northern Europe. Conveniently positioned for ships sailing from Hanseatic League harbours on the Continent, King's Lynn became England's pre-eminent port.

River Great Ouse ☆

2 Free Bridge **3** 1 mile

West bank, River Great Ouse

2 ▶ **Cross** the bridge, keeping to the right-hand pavement, and go through a fence gap to reach the embankment-top footpath on the far side.

3 ▶ Turn **right** onto the grassy path running along the top of an embankment beside the river.
▶ In ¾ mile the path becomes concrete and then a raised walkway leads to a ferry terminal.

NATURE NOTES

Knot

Thanks to the nearby Snettisham RSPB reserve just along the coast, the sky may be dotted with enormous flocks of knot and dunlin. Dunlins are the most common of Britain's small waders and, like the knot, are very gregarious. Additionally, up to 40,000 pink-footed geese come to this stretch of coastline in winter.

At around 3 feet from bill to tail, cormorants are large waterbirds. Fascinatingly, for a swimming and diving bird, cormorants' plumage is not waterproof and so they often sit with their wings outstretched to dry them.

Ferry Terminal (west bank)

2 miles

1½ miles

West bank, River Great Ouse

4 ▶ When invited to do so by the skipper, walk down the steps to the ferry and pay on board (there's a waiting room if the weather is inclement).

5 ▶ On the far bank, climb the steps and walk **ahead** along an alleyway, Ferry Lane, to the T-junction at the end.

6 ▶ At the junction, turn **left** for the Tuesday Market Place (75 yards).
▶ Otherwise, turn **right** along the pavement on King Street until you reach Purfleet Quay by the old Custom House (now an art gallery) in about 150 yards.

The tidal river and its wider environment provide good birdwatching opportunities. For instance, keep an eye on the ruined pier as you walk towards the ferry and you may see motionless herons.

Above left: heron
Above right: dunlin

If you're catching the ferry towards dusk, look seawards and you may glimpse a beautiful white barn owl hunting along the river.

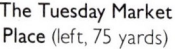

7 ▶ Turn **right** to walk over the cobbles to the riverside.

8 ▶ Turn **left** to walk along South Quay for ¼ mile.
▶ Follow the road as it swings sharply **left** and the car park lies ahead on the **right**.

Walk 1 King's Lynn   19

WALK 2

OLD HUNSTANTON

Given the prefix 'Old' to distinguish it from the brash 'new' purpose-built seaside resort to the west, this tiny village is packed with interest, from its associations with St Edmund and PG Wodehouse to its violent smuggling history. This walk takes in beach huts, a stretch of the River Hun and a golf course, before its leisurely return along the open sandy expanses of Old Hunstanton beach. There's an RNLI station to visit and a cheery beach café en route.

OS information
TF 679423
Explorer 250

Distance
3.4 miles/5.5km

Time
2 hours

Start/Finish
Old Hunstanton

Parking PE36 6EL
Clifftop car park

Public toilets
Old Hunstanton Beach, near ❾; Holme next the Sea, between ❺ and ❻; at the western end of Clifftop car park

Cafés/pubs
Old Town Beach Café, at ❷; The Mariner Inn, near ❸

Terrain
Pavement; sandy and earth tracks; sandy beach

Hilliness
Level throughout

Footwear
Spring/Autumn/Winter 🥾
Summer 👟

Public transport
Bus services 33, 34, 35 between King's Lynn and Hunstanton, and 36 Coastliner between King's Lynn, Wells-next-the-Sea and Fakenham: lynxbus.co.uk

20 Short Walks Made Easy

Accessibility
Not suitable for wheelchairs or pushchairs

Dogs
Welcome but keep on leads when crossing the golf course. No stiles

Did you know? PG Wodehouse reputedly typed out his stories on a punt on Hunstanton Hall moat (see p23). A friend of owner Charles Le Strange, the author featured the country house in his 1928 novel *Money for Nothing* and his short story compendium *Very Good, Jeeves*. The hall also served as the model for Anchorstone Hall in the novel *The Shrimp and the Anemone* by LP Hartley (of 'The past is a foreign country' fame).

Local legend Between Old Hunstanton Lighthouse (see p22) and the ruins of St Edmund's Chapel there sits a wolf of solid oak howling at the sky. The statue pays homage to the legend that a wolf guarded the body of St Edmund after he was killed by Norse invaders because he refused to renounce his Christian faith. The saint is said to have landed at Old Hunstanton on his way to becoming ruler of East Anglia in 855.

Walk 2 Old Hunstanton

STORIES BEHIND THE WALK

☆ Wreck of the steam trawler *Sheraton*

Given the proximity to the lighthouse of the remains of the *Sheraton*, it may be imagined the trawler was lost in some terrible storm. However, that's not the story at all. Launched in 1907, the *Sheraton* served in both world wars, on boom defence and coastal patrol. In 1945 she suffered the ignominy of being used as a practice target, was wrecked two years later while being towed and was then simply dumped.

☆ Old Hunstanton Lighthouse

It's believed a light was kept at St Edmund's chapel (now ruined) long before the first lighthouse was constructed on the clifftop here in 1665. When that burnt down a century or so later, a new wooden lighthouse was built, the first ever to use parabolic reflectors and the first major lighthouse to employ oil lamps rather than a coal brazier. The current trim building was erected in 1840 but decommissioned in 1921.

Clifftop car park

The Mariner Inn (right, 100 yards)

RNLI station (left) Old Town Beach Café

Golf Course Road

½ mile

1 ▶ Don't go down to the beach but take the first **right** off the main track along a narrower sandy path, passing an acorn symbol (left).

▶ Stay on this path as it wriggles along behind beach huts to an RNLI station in ¼ mile.

▶ Leave the car park at the end furthest from the lighthouse, by an exit marked with a large sign showing the rules for Old Hunstanton Beach.

☆ Pitched battle

On the night of 25 September 1784, a pitched battle between smugglers and customs officers of the 15th Light Dragoons took place at Old Hunstanton. Three excise men lost their lives in the pell-mell. The following year, the alleged killers were charged but acquitted for lack of evidence. The graves of two of the fallen officers, William Green and William Webb, can be seen in the nearby churchyard of St Mary the Virgin.

☆ Hunstanton Hall

This grand moated country house is a mishmash of different eras and styles. Only the gatehouse remains of the original building of 1487. In the 1620s, fine crenellated Jacobean ranges faced in flint were thrown up. The survivor of devastating fires in 1853 and 1950, the house is now divided into private apartments. In the 19th century, the owner of the hall, Henry L'Estrange Styleman Le Strange, founded neighbouring Hunstanton as a purpose-built tourist resort.

Hunstanton Golf Club

1 mile

River Hun

1½ miles

2 ➤ At the lifeboat station, turn **right** to go up a short lane to a multiple-road junction at the top.

3 ➤ Go sharp **left** to head along the shingly private Golf Course Road.
➤ After the houses, continue between the clubhouse and its car park and follow the road as it bends sharp **right** in ⅓ mile to a footpath and fingerpost (left).

Walk 2 Old Hunstanton 23

NATURE NOTES

One of Britain's shortest rivers, the Hun's journey of just a few miles begins in Hunstanton Park and ends in The Wash by Holme next the Sea. The stretch followed on this walk is little more than a stream bounding the golf course. A jumble of lush vegetation often hides it from view, but this is good habitat for mallard and teal.

River Hun

Top: mallard
Bottom: teal

Dunes — Broad sandy path along

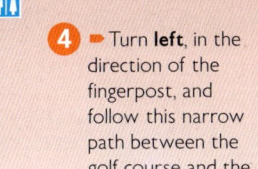

2 miles — 2½ miles

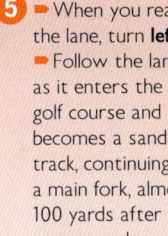

4 ➤ Turn **left**, in the direction of the fingerpost, and follow this narrow path between the golf course and the River Hun for almost 1 mile to meet a lane.

5 ➤ When you reach the lane, turn **left**.
➤ Follow the lane as it enters the golf course and becomes a sandy track, continuing to a main fork, almost 100 yards after the tarmac ends.

6 ➤ At the fork, take the **left-hand** path towards the dunes. In about 125 yards reach a fingerpost and a path turning on the left.

24 Short Walks Made Easy

In the dune slacks, if you are doing this walk at dusk in spring, you may be fortunate enough to hear the high-pitched whirring of the rare natterjack toad. They are nocturnal creatures and males call during the breeding season.

The damper dune slacks and wet grassland areas provide an ideal habitat for marsh helleborine, a stunning wetland orchid that can withstand the seasonal inundations that many other plants cannot. It flowers in July and August.

Little tern

Old Hunstanton beach offers visitors a mixture of sand and shingle backed by dunes. Birds you might see here include little tern and ringed plover.

he top of the beach

3 miles

Old Town Beach Café (ahead)

9 RNLI station

🅿 Clifftop car park

7 ▶ Ignore the turning and keep **forward** to pass through the dunes until you reach a wide sandy path at the top of a beach.

8 ▶ Turn **left** to walk along the top of the beach for 1.2 miles, straddling a number of low stone groynes along the way, to arrive at distinctive orange-topped posts, marking the lifeboat launch area.

9 ▶ At the posts, turn **left** towards the RNLI station.
▶ Retrace your outward steps by heading along the path beside the station and back to the car park.

Walk 2 Old Hunstanton 25

This page (clockwise): abandoned boat, Blakeney; Friary Hills, Blakeney; salt marsh, Wells-next-the-Sea; fingerpost at 6, Potter Heigham
Opposite (clockwise): North Norfolk Railway, Sheringham; mammoth sculpture, Sheringham; Captain George Vancouver, King's Lynn

WALK 3

WELLS-NEXT-THE-SEA

This linear route passes along wildlife-rich salt marshes and through England's largest national nature reserve. It also calls by The Lookout visitor centre, a stunning building with wonderful views over the reserve and interesting information about its flora and fauna. At the beach, a raised platform (accessible only by steps) has benches from where you can enjoy one of Norfolk's finest coastal vistas. The walk ends at Holkham Hall, well worth a visit before your return to Wells by bus.

OS information
TF 914437
Explorer 251

Distance
3.9 miles/6.25km

Time
2¼ hours

Start RCP car park, Wells-next-the-Sea
Finish Bus stop opposite entrance to Holkham Hall

Parking NR23 1AS RCP car park, Freeman Street, Wells-next-the-Sea

Public toilets Stearman's Yard car park, adjacent to car park at ⓐ; Beach Road, near ❷; at ❹, near RNLI station; Holkham village

Cafés/pubs Wells-next-the-Sea; Wells-next-the-Sea Beach Café at ❹; The Lookout, near ❻; The Victoria, by ❽; Courtyard Café, Holkham Hall

Terrain Pavement, tarmac and stony paths; boardwalk

Hilliness Level throughout, with a down ramp at ❸

Footwear Year round

 Public transport
Bus service 36 Coastliner between King's Lynn and Fakenham, with a bus stop at 🟠: lynxbus.co.uk

 Accessibility
Wheelchair and pushchair friendly

 Dogs Welcome but keep on leads on the beach from April to August. No stiles

Did you know? Despite the mile of salt marshes separating it from the North Sea, Wells has often found itself a victim of flooding since its emergence as a port in the 13th century. In recent times, the town was badly damaged in the catastrophic floods of 1953. Sixty years later, a storm surge battered Wells again, although at least that time the western side of town was saved by a tidal barrier constructed in 1982.

Local legend *A Haunting at Holkham* is a must-read novel for those who like a mix of spooky doings and stately homes. Written by Lady Glenconner, who grew up at Holkham Hall, the novel is inspired by the true story of Lady Mary Campbell who was imprisoned in Holkham for a year after spurning her husband on their wedding night. The author's sister has reportedly seen Mary's lonely ghost in her former room.

Walk 3 Wells-next-the-Sea

STORIES BEHIND THE WALK

🏛 **Holkham Hall** A magnificent 18th-century Palladian-style country house, Holkham Hall is surrounded by a huge and diverse estate that incorporates farmland, woodland, parkland and salt marsh. There's a deer park and an impressive six-acre walled garden to explore, a treetops rope walk to tackle, and a cycle-hire facility for cruising around the estate. Or you could hire a boat and row on the mile-long lake (holkham.co.uk).

☆ **Wells-next-the-Sea**

An important port since medieval times, Wells is a pretty little town that is very popular with tourists. Its history has been dominated by the salt marshes it faces and the difficulties involved in maintaining access through them to the sea. Over the centuries various engineers have attempted to create a permanent deep and wide channel and all have failed. Nowadays, sea traffic is largely reduced to pleasure boats and a fishing fleet that leaves and returns with the tides.

Wells-next-the-Sea ☆ | 🌲 Peddars Way and Norfolk Coast Path

½ mile

RCP car park, Wells-next-the-Sea

Wells Tide Recorder Station

Port of Wells private car park

Miniature Railway

▸ Leave the RCP car park by turning **right** out of the entrance along the pavement.
▸ **Cross** Glebe Road and, after another 25 yards, **cross** the main road to enter the Port of Wells private car park.

1 ▸ Walk towards the sea, with railings to your right, to the Wells Tide Recorder Station (WTRS), the raised building just up ahead.

30 Short Walks Made Easy

🚂 Wells & Walsingham Light Railway

Claiming to be the 'world's smallest public railway', the W&WLR takes a leisurely half-hour to chug the four miles from Wells to the village of Walsingham, famous for its pilgrimage abbey. On the way the little trains pass near an ancient hillfort and through some lovely Norfolk countryside. There's one stop along the route, at the village of Warham, where you can visit The Three Horseshoes, a delightful 300-year-old pub (wwlr.co.uk).

🐦 Holkham National Nature Reserve

There's an excellent mixture of habitats at Holkham, including salt marshes, creeks, dunes, pinewoods and a huge stretch of sandy beach. Bird enthusiasts may see oystercatchers and ringed plovers nesting in the dunes from March to August, and little terns diving into the sea after fish. Keep an eye out too for hares, and butterflies, such as the green hairstreak and the extraordinarily well-camouflaged grayling.

RNLI station   Wells-next-the-Sea Beach Café   ☕ Enter pine woodland   **Holkham National Nature Reserve**

mile   Pinewoods Holiday Park   1½ miles

🚩 **Peddars Way and Norfolk Coast Path**

2 ▶ Just past the WTRS, bear **right** to follow a tarmac path for 1 mile to the lifeboat station.

▶ Alternatively, walk along the top of the embankment instead by taking the steps to your **left** just after the WTRS and turn **right** at the top.

3 ▶ On reaching the RNLI station, turn **left** — almost back on yourself — to descend a concrete track (the pedestrian path to the left of the track offers a gentler descent).

Walk 3 Wells-next-the-Sea

NATURE NOTES

Woodland of Scots pine stands behind Holkham Beach and lines the route between ❺ and ❻.

And there's a rarity in the pine woods: an antlion. This is the only place in Britain, aside from the Suffolk coast, where this relative of the lacewing lives. It's so named because it pounces on ants that have fallen into the tiny craters it scrapes in the sand.

On the beach in summertime, you'll be serenaded by the high-pitched call of the oystercatcher. Scour the strand at low tide and you'll spot evidence of molluscs such as the razor shell, a bivalve that burrows vertically into the sand.

But before you reach the beach, pause a while at the lagoon, to your left (after ❺). In autumn and winter you may catch sight of the aptly named goldeneye duck or a little grebe bobbing to the surface after a lengthy swim underwater in search of food.

Holkham Lake

Opposite:
Top left: grayling
Top middle: little grebe
Top right: brown hare
Bottom right: razor shell

 Holkham National Nature Reserve

2 miles   2½ miles

Peddars Way and Norfolk Coast Path

❹ ▬ At the bottom, bear **right** following the Norfolk Coast Path acorn and NCN1 signs. Follow further signs to the seaward side of the car park to locate an entrance into pine woodland.

❺ ▬ Turn **left** to walk on a path between the pines. Follow occasional acorn/NCN1 signs, ignoring all side paths, along the Peddars Way and Norfolk Coast Path for 1¾ miles to reach The Lookout.

Antlion

The Lookout
☕ P V

The Lookout
☕ P V

Lady Anne's Drive

Holkham Beach

3 miles

3½ miles

Holkham Hall 🏛

The Victoria ☕

🚏

6 ➤ At The Lookout (left) – turn very sharply **right** onto a boardwalk between trees.
➤ Continue along this until it ends at Holkham Beach. Return by the same route.

7 ➤ Once you reach the intersection of paths by The Lookout again, turn **right** to walk down the wide Lady Anne's Drive. Carry on for ½ mile to the main road.

8 ➤ At the main road, turn **left** along the pavement to the bus stop for the bus back to the start.

WALK 4

BLAKENEY

It's extraordinary that, in this walk of just over two miles, you can experience three very distinct worlds. The first is a boat-lined harbour. A highly prosperous port in the Middle Ages, silt later made Blakeney's sea channels impassable to all but the lightest craft (many of which belonged to smugglers). Next there's the National Trust Friary Hills, where the air was once filled with the chanting of monks. Thirdly, there's the open expanse of Fresh Marshes with a big sky and an unpredictable sea beyond.

OS information
TG 026440 Explorer 251

Distance
2.3 miles / 3.7 km
Time
1½ hours
Start/Finish
Blakeney
Parking NR25 7NF The Quay (Westgate Street end); alternative car parks on Langham Road (NR25 7PG) and High Street (NR25 7NS)
Public toilets Back Lane (opposite ❶ and ❼)
Cafés/pubs Blakeney
Terrain Pavement; grassy paths and earth track; embankment top
Hilliness One brief ascent and descent in Friary Hills ❸ to ❹
Footwear Spring/Autumn/Winter Summer

Public transport
Bus service CH1, Coasthopper, between Cromer and Wells-next-the-Sea: sanderscoaches.com

Accessibility
Wheelchair and pushchair friendly in Blakeney, ① to ②, and on the embankment top, ⑥ to end

Dogs
Welcome but keep on leads in Friary Hills (NT) entered at ②. No stiles

Did you know? For centuries there was a thriving friary at Blakeney. Founded in 1296 by local lord Sir William Roos, brothers from the Carmelite Order set to work building themselves a friary (it took 25 years) and praying for the soul of their benefactor. The religious house prospered and grew until 1538, when Henry VIII had it dissolved. The farmhouse at Friary Farm, which incorporates some of the old buildings, is now a holiday let.

Local legend At dusk, the salt marshes are patrolled by Hyter Sprites (or Hikey Sprites) – arachnid-like creatures that scurry about on long legs or take to the air on weather-beaten wings. They enjoy sucking the blood of the unwary and snatching up children who stray onto the marshes after dark. It must be said that this latter behaviour comes in suspiciously handy for parents keen to scare their children out of night-time wanderings.

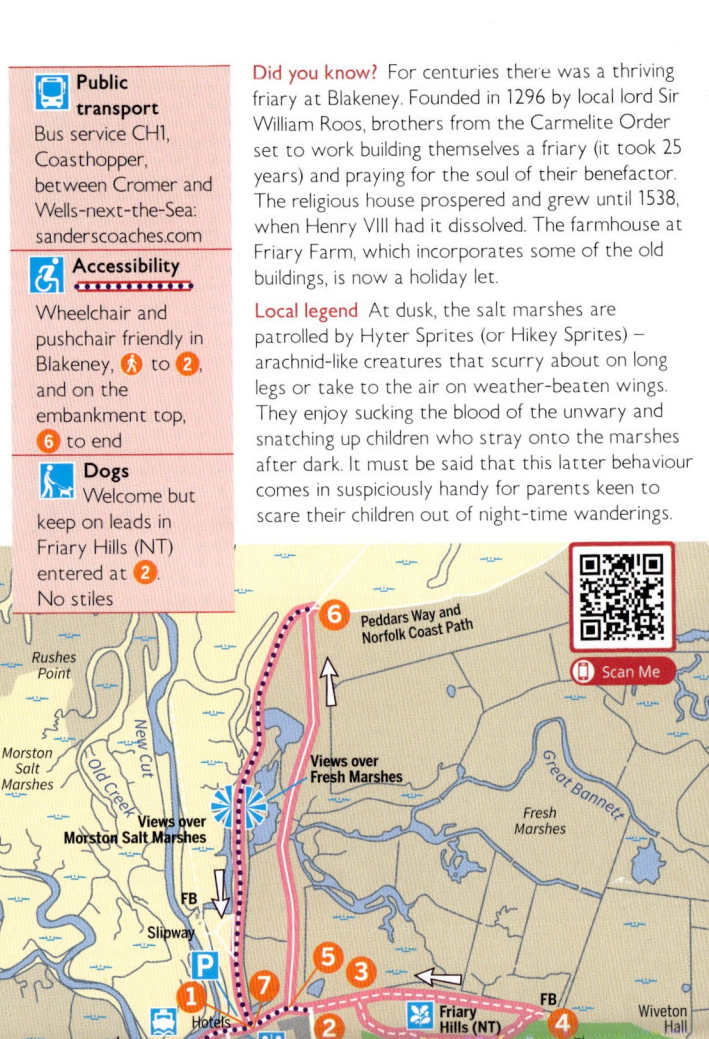

Walk 4 Blakeney

STORIES BEHIND THE WALK

☆ **The wreck of the *Hjørdis*** On 16 February 1916, the steamer SS *Hjørdis* – bound for Calais, laden with coal and crewed by ten Norwegians and a Dane –

ran aground on Blakeney Bar during a violent storm. One sailor, Ralf Petersen, tore off most of his clothing and swam for shore. He then staggered two miles along the beach to raise the alarm. The lifeboat was launched but no one else was saved. The wreck is still out on the bar, all but buried by sand, but now marked with a beacon.

Blakeney Point seals At the turn of the century there were just 25 seal pups born on Blakeney Point National Nature Reserve, a peninsula jutting off the coast at Blakeney. Today, it plays host to the largest colony of grey seals in England, with around of 4,500 pups expected in the 2023/24 season. By far the best way to view the colony is by booking with one of the boat tour operators who sail from nearby Morston Quay (for example, sealtrips.co.uk).

Guildhall (right)
The Quay — ❶ Cairn — ❷ Back Lane — ❸ Kissing-gate — Friary Hills — ½ mile

Peddars Way and Norfolk Coast Path

The Quay car park

▶ From the western end of The Quay, walk along the promenade towards Blakeney Hotel.

▶ Continue **ahead** past a car park (susceptible to flooding at high tide) to a cairn (left) overlooking a pond.

❶ ▶ Pass the cairn and carry on **ahead** on a roadside path for another 200 yards to a sharp right-hand bend.

36 Short Walks Made Easy

🏛 **Guildhall** The origins of Blakeney's Guildhall are swathed in mystery. The best guess is that it was a prosperous trader's home before becoming the headquarters of Blakeney's fish merchants in the early 16th century. Since then it's served as an inn (possibly), a coal store and, during World War I, a mortuary for drowned sailors. Now in the care of English Heritage, visitors are free to look over its stark exterior and peer into the gloomy undercroft, with its fine ribbed-brick vaulting (english-heritage.org.uk).

☆ **Blakeney Tower Windmill**
It may have been shorn of its sails but the Grade II-listed Blakeney Tower Windmill still stands proudly above the cottage roofs of the village. Built in 1769, it's believed to be the oldest of Norfolk's surviving corn windmills. The Gothic arches above doors and windows – an unusual feature – are a later addition. The windmill is owned by the National Trust who use it to accommodate staff and volunteers.

④ Kissing-gate Fingerpost ⑤

🌿 Friary Hills

1 mile

② ▶ As the road bends right, by a large flint building, bear **left** to pass through a kissing-gate and enter the National Trust's Friary Hills site.
▶ Keep forwards to a path junction in 100 yards.

③ ▶ Turn **right** onto a broad grassy path, heading upwards and along a low ridge (old friary's flint wall, right).
▶ Further on, enjoy the panorama across the marshes from a bench (left).
▶ Descend steps to reach a junction at the foot of the ridge.

NATURE NOTES

The grey seals on Blakeney Point are the stars of the show here. The pupping season, which lasts from November through to January, is a winter spectacle. The National Trust works year round to ensure that Blakeney Point remains a favourable environment for the seals.

However, there are plenty of other forms of nature to enjoy and look out for as well. Flocks of fieldfares alight on Fresh Marshes – they're known as the royal thrush in Spain due to their apparently regal demeanour and opulent colouring.

Heading out onto the marsh in the springtime, you might see yellow wagtails darting around the grazing cattle. And plenty of mute swans enjoy the labyrinth of watery channels and dykes that spread out across the marsh.

Up on the Friary Hills ridge, the bright yellow flowers of gorse are out almost all year and catch the eye as you look out over the marshes. In October, the sweet chestnut trees on the ridge provide foragers, both human and animal, with delicious provender.

Top: mute swans
Middle: fieldfare
Bottom: gorse

4 ▶ Turn **left** at the bottom and follow the grassy way back to the entrance gate.
▶ Retrace your steps towards the village, walking to a fingerpost and a turning on the right, opposite the Manor Hotel.

5 ▶ Go **right** along the track, signposted Restricted Byway.
▶ Continue on this track across the marshland for ½ mile to a kissing-gate.

Above: sweet chestnut tree
Below: sweet chestnuts

Top: Fresh Marshes
Bottom: grey seal pup

※ Views over Fresh Marshes (left) and Morston Salt Marshes (right)　　The Quay　　🚻 🏛 **Guildhall** (left)

2 miles　🌲 **Peddars Way and Norfolk Coast Path**　🅿 The Quay car park

6 ➤ Go through the kissing-gate, up onto a low embankment and turn **left** along a broad track.
➤ Follow it back to Blakeney (views over Fresh Marshes, left, and Morston Salt Marshes, right).

7 ➤ Upon reaching the road, turn **right** by a car park to return to The Quay.

Walk 4 Blakeney　39

Opposite (clockwise): black-headed gull; Chinese water deer; sycamore tree
This page (clockwise): avocet; grey seals; bearded tit; antlion larva

WALK 5

SHERINGHAM TO WEST RUNTON

With its slightly old-fashioned High Street leading down to an expansive sandy beach, it's easy to see why Sheringham is so popular with holidaymakers. This linear walk between railway stations takes you through the town, along the promenade and up onto Beeston Bump, a hillock affording 360-degree views. A clifftop walk leads to West Runton's Blue Flag beach, where the discovery of a mammoth once caused a sensation. You'll end at West Runton, with its handy cafés and train station.

OS information

TG 158430
Explorer 252

Distance
2.7 miles/4.25km

Time
1½ hours

Start Sheringham Railway Station
Finish West Runton Railway Station

Parking NR26 8RG Station Approach car park

Public toilets
Sheringham: Station Approach, High Street, Promenade; West Runton: beach

Cafés/pubs
Sheringham, West Runton and West Runton beach

Terrain
Pavement and concrete; sandy, grassy and tarmac paths

Hilliness
Steps down to the promenade ❸ and up again ❹; one brief ascent onto Beeston Bump ❺ to ❻

Footwear
Year round

Public transport
Sheringham and West Runton have mainline railway services: nationalrail.co.uk; bus services include CH1 and CH2 Coasthopper between Sheringham and Wells-next-the-Sea, and Cromer, Mundesley and North Walsham: sanderscoaches.com

Accessibility
Wheelchair and pushchair friendly to ❸ and ❼ to end

Dogs
Welcome. Keep on leads. No stiles

Did you know? The pelvis bone of a steppe mammoth was discovered in 1990 on West Runton's beach by two locals who had gone for a stroll. When more bones were revealed after a storm, an official excavation was organised and much of the 700,000-year-old creature's skeleton was recovered. It remains the most complete mammoth ever found in Britain. An imposing model of the animal stands near the beach to commemorate the discovery.

Local legend Stories about Black Shuck abound in East Anglia — a huge hound that roams the countryside spreading terror. In Sheringham, the tale goes that the creature lives on Beeston Bump, the hillock just to the east of the town. It's believed that Sir Arthur Conan Doyle was told of the beast during a holiday here in 1901 and was thus inspired to write *The Hound of the Baskervilles*.

Walk 5 Sheringham to West Runton

STORIES BEHIND THE WALK

☆ Sheringham's annual 1940s Event

For a long weekend every September, Sheringham steps back into the 1940s. The event was dreamed up by the North Norfolk Railway (see p45) to drum up custom but has since taken on a life of its own, engulfing Sheringham and drawing an estimated 40,000 visitors. The pubs are full of bands playing Glen Miller tunes, shops create elaborate window displays, the local theatre puts on '40s sing-alongs and hundreds roam the streets in intricate costumes from the era (experiencesheringham.com).

☆ Ancient West Runton

The discoveries of prehistoric iron-ore pits and a set of quern stones from the Roman era suggest the West Runton area has long been a popular centre of human activity. Some 600,000 years ago, rhinos roamed here and, even further back, there were steppe mammoths (see p43). The beach and cliffs are prone to erosion caused by winter storms, making them a paradise for (careful) fossil-hunters. Unsurprisingly, West Runton now forms part of the Deep History Coastal Trail (north-norfolk.gov.uk).

North Norfolk Railway — Station Road — High Street — **Sheringham Museum at The Mo** — Promenade — Steps — ½ mile — **East Beach Coffee** — Steps — **Beeston Hills Putting Green**

Sheringham Railway Station

➤ Exit Sheringham station and turn **right** to stroll down Station Road to its junction with High Street in 300 yards.

1 ➤ On meeting High Street, continue **ahead**, ignoring all side turnings to reach the sea wall in just under 250 yards.

2 ➤ Turn **right** and walk to The Mo (Sheringham Museum).

🚂 North Norfolk Railway

The optimism with which railways were built in Norfolk in the 19th century can be measured in the number of disused lines there today. A smattering have been partly restored as heritage railways (see Walks 3 and 6). The North Norfolk Railway, for example, stretches just over five miles from Sheringham to Holt. Extremely scenic, its stations and trains have starred in many a television programme, including the BBC's *Dad's Army* and *Love on a Branch Line* (nnrailway.co.uk).

🏛 Sheringham Museum at The Mo

Built on the seafront on top of a huge storm and overflow tank, this curiously named museum with its quirky lookout tower is definitely worth a stop on your way. Its exhibits range from flint arrow heads to a fisherman's cottage. But pride of place goes to the historic fishing boats and four (of the five) lifeboats that served the town from 1894 through to 1990 (sheringhammuseum.co.uk).

 Norfolk Coast Path

 Beeston Bump — ❻ Trig point — 1 mile

Beeston Regis Holiday Park 🚐

❸ ▶ **Descend** the steps and continue for 350 yards along the promenade, passing the toilets and beach huts, to reach a flight of steps (right) immediately after East Beach Coffee.

❹ ▶ **Climb** the steps. At the top of the flight, walk up the broad concrete way to a lane and tall fingerpost (left) by Beeston Hills Putting Green.

Walk 5 Sheringham to West Runton

NATURE NOTES

Look out to sea as you head along this clifftop walk and you could spot Britain's largest seabird, the gannet, gliding about the sky or performing one of its lightning-fast dives into the water after fish. Above the cliffs another hunter hovers – the kestrel. If you're lucky, you may hear or even spot a kestrel's favourite prey, the field vole, scurrying about the tussocky grass attempting to evade the raptor's attention.

The common mallow adds some shades of mauve to the scene. It's a close relative of marsh mallow from which the dye was once extracted to colour the pink sweets of the same name. Brambles and their blackberry fruit supply a rather healthier sweet snack in the late summer and autumn. And just before you reach the Water Lane car park at **7**, look for the extensive patches of purple sorrel.

Common mallow

Marsh mallow

Purple sorrel

Norfolk Coast Path

1½ miles

Laburnum Caravan Park

5 ▶ Go **left**, passing the putting green, keeping **ahead** for a few yards to reach the beginning of a narrow sandy footpath; the Norfolk Coast Path.

▶ Follow the coast path for ¼ mile to the trig point on top of Beeston Bump.

6 ▶ Continue **forward** across the summit and stay on the coast path for more than a mile to a small car park at West Runton beach.

▶ You'll stay close to the clifftop edge – take care, there is a fence – passing two holiday parks.

46 Short Walks Made Easy

Gannets mate for life

Bramble

Above: kestrel
Below: field vole

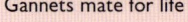

☆ Mammoth sculpture ... Ancient West Runton ☆ ... Station Road

Water Lane — 2½ miles

West Runton beach — West Runton Railway Station

7 ▸ Pass through the small car park and turn **right** up Water Lane.
▸ Remain on the lane as it kinks to the left to reach a main road in just over ⅓ mile.

8 ▸ Bearing **right** at the junction, **cross** the road carefully and head along Station Road (almost opposite).
▸ This will take you the 350 yards to West Runton station for the train back to Sheringham.

WALK 6

BUXTON

This route begins with a gentle stroll between two stations of the Bure Valley Railway, a miniature line whose creation funded the construction of the footpath that runs alongside it. You'll then switch to a path beside the River Bure, once important as a trade route, before making a detour to the historic Oxnead Hall and St Michael & All Angels' Church, whose nave dates back to the time of Edward the Confessor. Lastly, there's a pleasant amble back across fields.

OS information
TG 231229
Explorers 238, OL40

Distance
2.8 miles/4.5km

Time
1¾ hours

Start/Finish
Buxton

Parking NR10 5ET
Bure Valley Walk car park

Public toilets
None

Cafés/pubs
The Black Lion, Buxton

Terrain
Lane; and gravel, earth, concrete and grassy paths

Hilliness
Gently undulating; steps down at ❷ and ❺

Footwear
Winter 🥾
Spring/Summer/Autumn 👟

Public transport
Bus service 54 between Norwich and North Walsham: sanderscoaches.com; Bure Valley Railway (narrow gauge) between Wroxham and Aylsham, with the station at ⓘ: bvrw.co.uk

48 Short Walks Made Easy

Accessibility
Wheelchair and pushchair friendly from 🚶 to ❷ (and on the lane ❸ to ❺)

Dogs
Welcome but keep on leads when crossing the railway. No stiles

Did you know? The Bure Valley Railway (see p50) has taken a leading role in the development and trial of 'e-coal' for use by heritage railways. Made from a combination of coal dust and waste biomass from the production of olive oil – both of which normally go to landfill – the e-coal has been found to reduce carbon dioxide emissions by 42 per cent when compared with burning standard coal.

Local legend In a story surprisingly similar to that of the apparition at Potter Heigham (see p63), Buxton too has a phantom coach crossing a bridge once a year on a specific night. Every 19 May, a ghostly coach and four can be seen driven by a headless coachman. He is said to be Sir Thomas Boleyn, who takes this journey over no fewer than 11 bridges every year on the anniversary of his daughter Anne's beheading.

Walk 6 Buxton 49

STORIES BEHIND THE WALK

Bure Valley Railway For 73 years, from 1879, the locals were served by Buxton Lamas railway station which stood on a Great Eastern Railway branch line. Since 1990, the 15-inch minimum gauge Bure Valley Railway has run on nine miles of the original trackbed connecting Wroxham to Aylsham, stopping at Buxton on the way. The railway attracts more than 100,000 passengers a year and is a fun way of reaching the start of this walk (bvrw.co.uk).

☆ River Bure

Flowing 32 miles from source to sea, the Bure is the longest of the Broadland rivers. Today, it's navigable from its mouth at Gorleston (near Great Yarmouth) up through Acle and Wroxham to Coltishall. In the 18th century, a great deal of money was spent on locks and improvements to allow trading vessels to sail upstream to Buxton and as far as Aylsham, carrying flour, coal, timber and crops. A catastrophic flood in 1912 put paid to the venture.

½ mile

Bure Valley Path

Bure Valley

Buxton Station

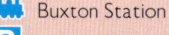

Bure Valley Walk car park

➤ From the car park, head beneath the metal demi-arch and cross the railway line, looking both ways for trains.

1 ➤ Turn immediately **left** along the trackside path (Bure Valley Path) and follow it for nearly a mile to Brampton Station.

2 ➤ At the little station, turn **right** to descend two flights of steps to a lane.

50 Short Walks Made Easy

🏠 Oxnead Hall

Although it was the seat of the enormously wealthy Paston family from 1420, the current house was built around 1580 by Sir Clement Paston amid a vast estate. The hall was expanded 50 years later, making Oxnead one of East Anglia's most imposing stately homes. Though much was torn down in the 18th century, following the collapse of the family's fortunes, the hall remains impressive. It now serves as a family home and an upmarket wedding venue.

☆ **Paston family letters** Correspondences between members of high-born families were not unusual in medieval times. However, the stash of over a thousand letters written between 1418 and 1509 by members of the Paston family of Oxnead Hall and their associates is the only collection in English known to have survived from that period. As such, it has proved an invaluable primary source of information for historians and linguists (thisispaston.co.uk).

3 ▸ Turn **left** along the lane to the road junction in 100 yards.

4 ▸ At the junction turn **right** along Marsham Road.
▸ Continue **ahead** to the left of the Bramtuna sign, ignoring a right turn to Norwich, and carrying on along the road to a bridge in 300 yards.

NATURE NOTES

As you head along the Bure Valley Railway ⟨🚶⟩ to ②, look out for orpine, a large succulent bearing dense heads of deep-red flowers far into autumn, and dock, the friend to all who have been stung by nettles (its alkaline juices counteract the stinging nettle's prickling acids).

The River Bure may look peaceful today but in the 18th century its course was liberally redirected to allow wherries to carry goods. A terrible flood in 1912 destroyed the locks and bridges and silted the river up.

Keep a look out for blackthorn shrubs, especially in autumn when their attractive blue-black sloes ripen; and sycamore, a species of maple beloved for its propeller-guided seeds. In the copse (entered at ⑧) you may hear a great spotted woodpecker tapping away at a tree before you see it.

River Bure

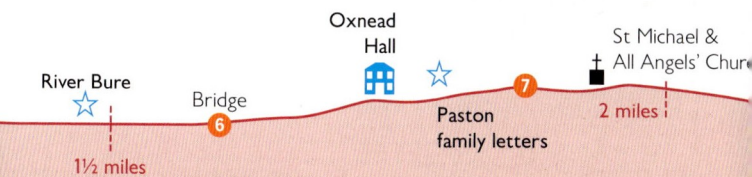

⑤ ▪ At the bridge, immediately before it crosses the Bure, turn **right** down steps onto a riverside path.
▪ Follow the riverside path for ⅓ mile to a kissing-gate.

⑥ ▪ Go through the gate and turn **left** over a bridge.
▪ Head up the track, which bends left. Continue over an expanse of concrete and round the back of Oxnead Hall to an unsigned track on the left.

Short Walks Made Easy

Great spotted woodpecker

Orpine

Above: stinging nettle
Below: dock

Bridge — Copse — 2½ miles — Buxton Station

Bure Valley Walk car park

7 ▸ Go **left** along the track by an estate wall (left).
▸ This leads to the interesting St Michael & All Angels' Church. After visiting, retrace your steps to the bridge (crossed after **6**).

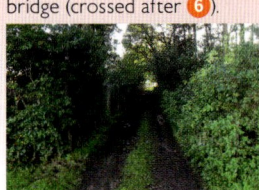

8 ▸ **Cross** the bridge and continue **straight ahead** through a copse and then follow a clear field-edge path back to Buxton Station.

Walk 6 Buxton

WALK 7

TOAD HOLE

Striking out from Ludham, with its impressive church and welcoming pub set in a delightful corner of the Broads, this walk is packed with interest: there's Toad Hole Cottage, a rare and authentic marshman's abode now turned into a small museum; a chance to visit some glorious gardens – one formal and one 'secret' – and How Hill staithe, from where you can take an electric boat for a wildlife-watching trip along a beautiful stretch of the River Ant.

OS information
TG 388183 Explorer OL40
Distance 3.75 miles/6km
Time 2¼ hours
Start/Finish Ludham
Parking NR29 5QA Lay-by opposite the King's Arms, Norwich Road
Public toilets How Hill (seasonal, after ⑤)
Cafés/pubs King's Arms, Ludham; Toad Hole Cottage (takeaway snacks)
Terrain Lanes and pavement; grass verge and field paths
Hilliness Mostly level; one gentle climb from the River Ant ⑤ to ⑥
Footwear Winter 🥾 Spring/Summer/Autumn 👟
Public transport Bus services 6 and X6 between North Walsham, Stalham and Great Yarmouth: sanderscoaches.com; and 5B between Norwich, Wroxham and Stalham: konectbus.co.uk

Accessibility
Wheelchair and pushchair friendly (crossing grass at ③) from 🚶 to ⑥, and ⑨ to end

Dogs
Welcome but keep on leads. No stiles

Did you know? Nature reserves may seem more or less timeless but the one at How Hill has very much entered the 21st century. Bring your phone along and you can take advantage of some augmented reality. Information about the reserve will appear, as if by magic, on your screen depending on your precise location, helping you to a deeper understanding of this invaluable ecosystem. See Toad Hole Cottage, p56, for details.

Local legend Ludham may look peaceful now but there was a time when a dragon added spice to the villagers' lives. It dug a series of tunnels below their houses, emerging at night to terrify one and all. Then, one day, when the creature was enjoying a rare sunbathe, a villager blocked up its tunnel entrance. The maddened dragon took out its wrath on nearby St Benet's Abbey before establishing a new home beneath its gatehouse.

Walk 7 Toad Hole

STORIES BEHIND THE WALK

Toad Hole Cottage In Victorian times, a marshman's job would have involved, among other tasks, trimming and cutting reeds and tending the cattle that grazed on the marshes – steady work but not well paid. This museum, set inside a marshman's cottage, takes visitors back to that era to give them a fascinating insight into the world of the marshman and his family in their rather cramped conditions (broads-authority.gov.uk).

How Hill Trust Garden and Secret Garden An independent educational charity that runs the Environmental Study Centre for the Broads, the How Hill Trust tends a calming formal garden (open when no students are at the centre) and a 'secret garden' in How Hill Wood (open daily). Both were created by architect Edward Boardman in the 1920s. Visit the Secret Garden in late spring/early summer for the colourful rhododendrons and azaleas, and in autumn for golden leaves. Entrance is by donation (howhilltrust.org.uk).

1 ► **Cross** the High Street to go down School Road.
► Ignore all turnings off School Road through the village. Keep **forwards** at a staggered crossroads to the next lane junction in 350 yards.

► Head along the pavement on the right-hand side of the High Street, passing the King's Arms (left), to a crossroads in 200 yards.

2 ► At the junction, turn **right** and follow the lane for just over ¾ mile to the How Hill site entrance.

Short Walks Made Easy

☆ Romans and Saxons on the River Ant

At just 17 miles, the Ant may not be the longest of rivers, but it has quite a history of human activity. In 1976, road-builders dug up remnants of a Roman boat and a wooden causeway near Wayford Bridge, 6 miles upstream of Ludham. Two Saxon boats have also been discovered. Both dug-out canoes, one has been dated to CE 720, making it Norfolk's oldest known vessel. The other can be seen at Norwich Castle Museum (museums.norfolk.gov.uk/norwich-castle).

🚤 Electric Eel Wildlife Water Trail

Have you ever been in a boat on a river, yearning to get close to wildlife, only to see it scuttle or fly away at the sound of the engine? Then the Electric Eel is for you. Designed to glide along the River Ant's many shallow dykes with Ninja-like stealth, the elegant open-sided boat has an extremely quiet electric motor. The result is a deeper look into the doings of the river's wildlife. Tickets are available from Toad Hole Cottage (Easter to September).

③ ▶ Turn **left**, following the sign to Toad Hole Cottage and immediately bear **right** through a car park and then slightly **right** again across a grassy field to its far side.

▶ The How Hill Trust formal gardens are to your right.

④ ▶ At the far end of the field, continue on a path leading quickly down to Toad Hole Cottage.

▶ After visiting, continue to the River Ant, to a staithe (landing stage). Walk to its **right-hand** end.

NATURE NOTES

The area beside the River Ant is one of the few places in England where you might see a swallowtail butterfly, whose large size and bright colours are always a delight to behold. A full-grown swallowtail caterpillar is also brightly coloured. The larvae feed on milk parsley, angelica or wild carrot.

Meanwhile, white dead nettle provides food for all sorts of insects. You can amaze children by brushing your hands against its barb-free stinging nettle-like leaves too.

You'll find apple trees in the small orchard beside Toad Hole Cottage. In How Hill's formal gardens, meanwhile, are more exotic plants such as figs and huge stands of pampas grass, the latter an import from South America, and particularly from the vast Pampas region after which it is named. But perhaps the most unusual plant is the glorytree, which comes from Asia. Its ripe fruits (called drupes) are bright blue amidst pink petals, and its leaves smell of peanuts when crushed.

Swallowtail

How Hill National Nature Reserve

5 ► At the staithe's end, turn **right**, following a public footpath fingerpost.
► Continue on this track, past How Hill House and back to the lane.
► Turn **left** and walk to a grassy track (right, opposite a house, left) in 350 yards.

6 ► Turn **right** on the grassy path, passing between a line of trees and a hedge.
► **Carry on** for ¼ mile to a path junction and waymarker post, ignoring a turning off to the left halfway along.

Short Walks Made Easy

Above: swallowtail larva
Below: angelica

Top: glorytree
Bottom: pampas grass

Goffins Lane (crossing) — 3 miles
Catfield Road — 3½ miles
King's Arms, High St
Lay-by, Norwich Road (opposite pub)

7 ► Take the footpath to your **right**. In another ¼ mile bear **right** as a path joins from the left and reach a path T-junction in 50 yards.

8 ► Turn **left**. In 350 yards, **cross** Goffins Lane and **carry on** for about ⅓ mile to reach Catfield Road.

9 ► Turn **right** along the wide grass verge, and then pick up the pavement to return to the King's Arms.

COFFEE TO
COCKTAILS
THE GANGWAY

The
Victoria

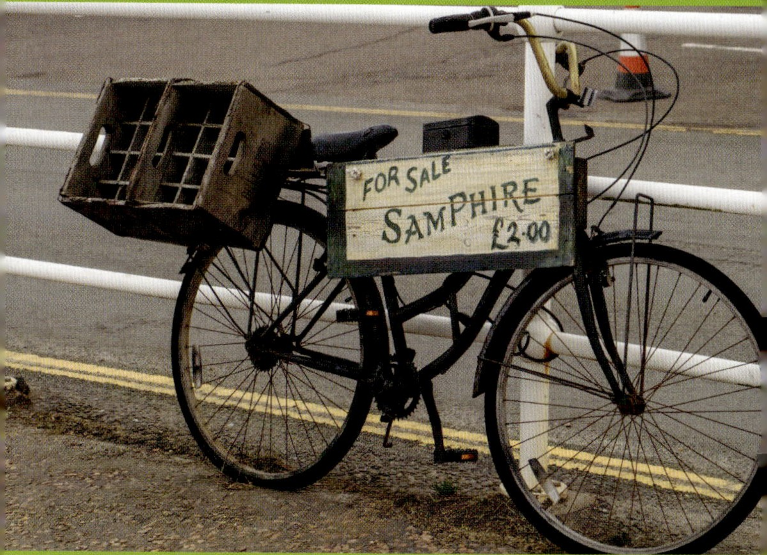
FOR SALE
SAMPHIRE
£2.00

Breakfast
Lunch
Afternoon Tea

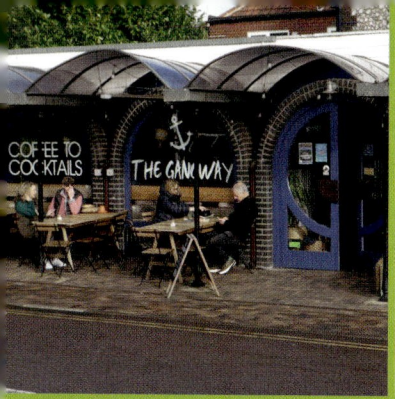

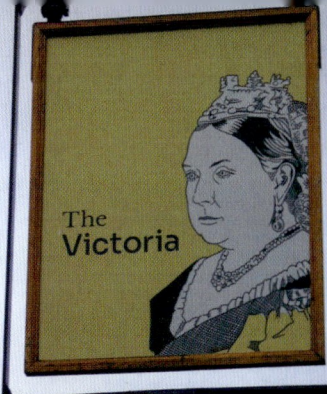

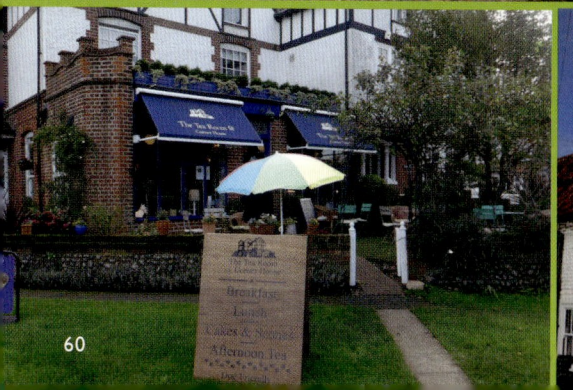

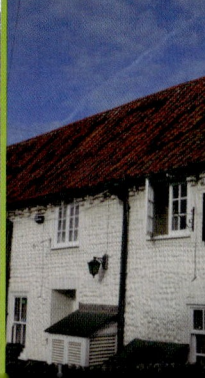

Opposite (clockwise):
The Gangway, Sheringham;
The Victoria, Holkham;
samphire for sale in Blakeney;
The Tea Room at Corner House, West Runton
This page (clockwise):
Falgate Inn, Potter Heigham;
Birdys Bakehouse, Blakeney;
Kings Arms, Blakeney

WALK 8

POTTER HEIGHAM

No one would blame you if you delayed setting off on this walk to look around the stunning medieval church at its start. A saunter across fields and through a wood then takes you to Hickling Broad — one of the largest expanses of water in East Anglia — for a splendid ramble along its southern shore before your return through more fields and woods. One word of caution: sections of this walk can get muddy and puddly after a lot of rain.

OS information

TG 419198
Explorer OL40

Distance
4.1 miles/6.6km

Time
2½ hours

Start/Finish
Potter Heigham

Parking NR29 5LL
St Nicholas's Church, Potter Heigham (not on grass bank)

Public toilets
None

Cafés/pubs
Falgate Inn, Potter Heigham

Terrain
Lanes; grassy field paths; earth paths and track

Hilliness
Level throughout

Footwear
Year round

Public transport
Bus services 6 and X6 between North Walsham, Stalham and Great Yarmouth: sanderscoaches.co.uk (bus stop on Bridge Road opposite Mill Road, ¾ mile from)

62 Short Walks Made Easy

Accessibility

In dry conditions, powered wheelchairs and all-terrain pushchairs from ④ to end via Marsh Road shortcut, and on lane ⓧ to ①

Dogs Keep on leads on lanes and on the Weavers' Way (path ③ to ④). No stiles

Did you know? Hickling Broad served as a Royal Naval Air Service (RNAS) seaplane reserve station during World War I. Pilots who found that choppy waters or bad weather prevented them from landing on the sea at the nearby Great Yarmouth base, could attempt to come down on Hickling Broad instead. The seaplanes were mostly used to combat Zeppelin airships sent over the Channel to bomb south-east England.

Local legend In 1742, a young woman called Evelyn is said to have enjoyed something of an unconventional wedding day: she was captured and taken away in a phantom coach driven by a skeleton. Passing over Potter Heigham Bridge (see p65), the coach burst into flames, or toppled into the river, depending on which story you believe. Happily, the ghostly coach can be seen every 31 May at midnight, so you could check yourself which version is true.

Walk 8 Potter Heigham

STORIES BEHIND THE WALK

✝ St Nicholas's Church With its round tower, thatched chancel and unusually tall clerestory (the section of windows above the nave), this is one of Norfolk's most aesthetically pleasing churches. It's also firmly set in the Middle Ages. The tower is 12th century, with a 14th-century octagonal extension, while its font — the only brick-built one in the county — is 15th-century. But its glory comes from the hammer-beam roof and medieval wall paintings. The church is usually open from dawn to dusk.

🐦 Hickling Broad The largest of the Norfolk Broads by surface area, Hickling Broad is very shallow — its navigable channel is a mere 5 feet deep. Along with Hickling Sound, Horsey Mere and Martham Broad, it forms a Site of Special Scientific Interest (SSSI). Its importance stems from its range of wetland plants such as the rare holly-leaved naiad. It's also home to England's largest reed bed.

✝ St Nicholas's Church   🐦 Hickling Broad

Church Lane — ① — ② — ③ — ½ mile — Weavers' Way — 1 mile

③ Hickling Broad Information Board

■ Head along Church Lane, with the church to your right, to where the lane bends sharply left in 250 yards.

① ■ At the bend, turn sharp **right** onto a bridleway with a hedge to your right. Continue to a path junction in 100 yards.

64 Short Walks Made Easy

⭐ *Coot Club* and *The Big Six*

Arthur Ransome is famous for his perennial children's classic *Swallows and Amazons*, based in the Lake District. However, he wrote another 12 novels in the same series, two of which were set in the Norfolk Broads. *Coot Club* follows the exploits of Dick and Dorothea Callum as they learn to sail despite the attentions of a group of inconsiderate city folk; while *The Big Six* takes the form of a thrilling detective story. Potter Heigham features in both.

⭐ Potter Heigham's sinking bridge

If you hire anything but a tiny boat on the Norfolk Broads, you can be sure of one thing: writ large in the instructions will be a stern warning: 'This boat will not pass under Potter Heigham Bridge'. Built around 1385 to aid travellers heading between Cromer and Great Yarmouth, the notorious three-arched bridge has gradually sunk over the centuries. It's now so low that only the smallest pleasure cruisers can slip beneath it, and then only at low tide.

Wagonhill Plantation (right) — Heigham Sound (left) — Sound Plantation (right) — Candle Dyke (left)

Deep-Go Dyke (left)

1½ miles

2 miles

2 ➤ At the junction, turn **left** on a footpath between a row of trees and a hedge.
➤ Carry on for 350 yards then enter woodland, very soon meeting a path junction and Hickling Broad information board.

3 ➤ Turn **left** at the information board.
➤ At Hickling Broad, in 225 yards, swing **right** to join the Weavers' Way. Follow its meandering course for 1½ miles to a path junction just before a metal five-bar gate (left).

Walk 8 Potter Heigham

NATURE NOTES

Birders love Hickling Broad and it's no wonder because it's a mecca for all sorts of avian life. A sizeable proportion of Britain's common crane population breeds here, along with Cetti's warbler, bittern, bearded tit, barn owl and kingfisher, among many others species. In winter, marsh harriers can be seen here too.

Otters inhabit the waters though it takes patience or a slice of luck to catch a glimpse of them. But you may spot some red deer or even some Chinese water deer with their endearing 'Mickey Mouse' ears.

On the way to Hickling Broad you'll see plenty of oak and ash trees, the latter a welcome sight given the terrible spread of ash dieback. And from July to October you'll be greeted by the cheerful mustard-yellow flowers of tansy.

Common crane

Return, left, along Marsh Road

Fingerpost

2½ miles

3 miles

4 ▸ Turn **right**, away from the broad, along a straight farm track between reeds.
▸ In just under ½ mile, watch for a turning on the right at a fingerpost.

5 ▸ At the Public Bridleway fingerpost, go **right** to reach a junction and lone house in ¼ mile.

Short Walks Made Easy

Top left: bittern
Left: marsh harrier
Top: oak leaves
Middle: ash leaves
Bottom: tansy

St Nicholas's Church ✝

3½ miles   4 miles

6 ➤ 🄰 For a shortcut, go **left** along the lane back to the church.

➤ Otherwise, keep **ahead** along the track, which narrows to a path, for ¾ mile to return to the Hickling Broad information board. Here go **left** to retrace your steps to the church.

Walk **8** Potter Heigham

WALK 9

WINTERTON-ON-SEA

CATCH A BUS

OS information
TG 498197
Explorer OL40

Distance
3.4 miles/5.4km

Time
2 hours

Start/Finish
Winterton-on-Sea

Parking NR29 4AJ
Winterton Beach car park

Public toilets
Opposite car park

Cafés/pubs
Dunes Café, at the car park; Poppy's Tea Room and Fishermans Return, Winterton-on-Sea

Terrain
Roads; grassy field paths and crushed-stone track

Hilliness
Gently undulating

Starting on a beach that has seen many a shipwreck – both real and fictional – this walk whisks you from wonderful dunes into the quiet seaside village of Winterton, beloved of novelists Daniel Defoe, Wilkie Collins and Sylvia Townsend Warner. Heading across fields, you're conveyed into an unassuming copse that harbours one of Norfolk's best-kept secrets: the evocative and somewhat eerie remains of a haunted church. You return to the beach where grey seals have their pups each autumn/winter.

Footwear
Year round

Public transport
Bus services 1 and 1A, Coastal Clipper, between Lowestoft, Caister-on-Sea and Martham (bus stops in Black Street and Bulmer Lane): firstbus.co.uk/norfolk-suffolk

Accessibility
Wheelchair and pushchair friendly from ⓧ to Hemsby Road ❷, and from High Barn Farm after ❹ to end

Dogs
Welcome but keep on leads on road sections. No stiles

Did you know? Wilkie Collins, the father of the detective story, visited Winterton-on-Sea in 1864 while preparing the notes for his novel *Armadale*. He had been drawn to the village because he was a great devotee of Daniel Defoe, whose hero Robinson Crusoe was first shipwrecked at Winterton. During his visit, the 40-year-old Collins met 19-year-old Martha Rudd, with whom he went on to have three children.

Local legend With its lofty stone walls consumed by the copse in which it stands, the ruined church of St Mary's in East Somerton is wonderfully atmospheric. Abandoned in the 1600s, legend has it that the single majestic oak that adorns the interior of the nave grew out of the wooden leg of a witch who was buried there to keep her evil spirit in check. Naturally enough, her shade is said to haunt the place.

Walk 9 Winterton-on-Sea 69

STORIES BEHIND THE WALK

Winterton Dunes NNR

A spectacular national nature reserve covering 270 acres, Winterton Dunes may appear similar to other dunes around the country but they're actually highly unusual. Rather than being alkaline, they're acidic – like dunes you'd find more readily on the Baltic coast. As a result, they harbour flora and fauna that are rare to these shores. They're also home to grey seals and nationally important colonies of natterjack toads and little terns.

Edward Fawcett

Winterton fisherman turned polar explorer, Edward Fawcett's Arctic experiences are the stuff of nightmares. In 1850, he sailed with HMS *Investigator* to try to save Sir John Franklin's expedition, which had gone missing in 1847, when *Investigator* became trapped by ice. After three years she was abandoned. The weakened crew trudged for a fortnight to another ship which also became trapped. It took another terrible frozen march to reach ships that would finally convey them back to Britain.

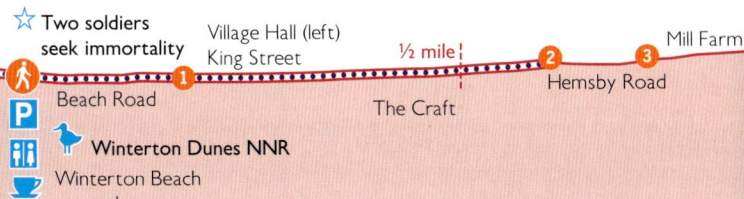

Winterton Dunes NNR
Winterton Beach car park

- From the car park, walk along the road, away from the sea, to the village hall and first road turning (left).

1
- Turn **left** onto King Street.
- At a crossroads in 200 yards, go **straight over** and keep **forwards** on The Craft for ¼ mile to the T-junction with Hemsby Road/Bulmer Lane.

☆ **Two soldiers seek immortality** The threat of invasion during World War II led to the placing of huge 13-ton anti-tank blocks amid the dunes at Winterton. Two soldiers taking part in the defence of this sector were Private Wells and Private Russell. We know this because they scratched their names into one block, with Wells adding the date: 18 September 1941. Now viewed by academics as an important historical artefact, the block and the names of Wells and Russell live on.

☆ Winterton Lighthouse

Notorious as a graveyard for shipping, this dangerous headland was afforded its first lighthouse — which employed a coal brazier — in the early 1600s. This was succeeded by a series of other lighthouses until the current building was erected in the 1860s. This served as a lookout tower in both world wars, between which it was decommissioned in favour of a light vessel. The lighthouse has since been converted into an unconventional holiday let (wintertonlighthouse.com).

2 ▶ Turn **left** along Hemsby Road.
▶ After 50 yards, pick up a grassy footpath that runs parallel to the road on the **right** and acts as a pavement. Continue to Mill Farm.

3 ▶ At the farm entrance, turn **right** on a gravel drive.
▶ Continue **forward** when the drive becomes a waymarked grass path between fields. Carry on for ½ mile to where the path bends sharp right.

4 ▶ Turn sharp **right** with the path, after which it becomes a track heading past High Barn Farm.
▶ This soon becomes a tarmac track and goes on for ½ mile to meet a road.

Walk 9 Winterton-on-Sea

NATURE NOTES

Although this walk begins on a beach backed by dunes, it quickly heads inland across an arable landscape where you might hear the song of the skylark as it ascends the heavens. You may also spot or startle pheasants, sending them noisily into the air. Along the field hedgerows and roadside verges, butterflies such as red admirals and peacocks are on the wing in summer.

There are hedges of hawthorn, a tree so common in much of Britain that it's generally unregarded but which adds glorious splashes of white blossom to the countryside in late spring and red berries later in the year. The guelder rose also produces a red berry but one that looks much more like a cranberry.

After a period of damp weather you may also see the shaggy inkcap poking up through the grass on the roadside verges. One of its other names is, for reasons that are obvious when you see it, 'lawyer's wig'.

Guelder rose

5 ▬ At the road, cross it carefully, jinking **left** and then **right** to head on down Manor Farm Road.
▬ After 300 yards, you can visit ghostly St Mary's Church (left). Afterwards, continue 25 yards to the road junction.

6 ▬ At the junction, turn **right** along Low Road, walking past Manor Farm.
▬ 200 yards beyond the farm, where Low Road bends sharply right, take the well-made crushed-stone track **ahead** (still Low Road).

72   Short Walks Made Easy

Skylark

Top: red admiral
Middle: peacock
Bottom: shaggy inkcap

Poppy's Tea Room

Two soldiers seek immortality ☆
Beach Road

3 miles
North Market Road

Winterton Dunes NNR

Winterton Beach car park

7 ► Ignoring all turnings off, stay on Low Road for ⅔ mile to its end at a T-junction.

8 ► At the T-junction, turn **right** along North Market Road for 250 yards, bending **right** near the end to go on to another T-junction.

9 ► Turn **left** along Beach Road, soon passing Poppy's Tea Room (right), to return to the beach car park.

Walk 9 Winterton-on-Sea 73

WALK 10

BURGH CASTLE

If you're keen to extend the list of things the Romans have done for us, you could add 'leaving a humungous wall in the Norfolk countryside'. This walk visits the mighty structure, once part of a cavalry fort. It overlooks the far western end of Breydon Water, an estuary that forms part of the Norfolk Broads. A long boardwalk section offers views over reed beds and mudflats where birdlife is abundant. And finally there's a hidden Saxon church to be discovered.

OS information
TG 481051
Explorer OL40

Distance
2.5 miles/4km

Time
1½ hours

Start/Finish
Burgh Castle (arriving by bus – Queen's Head bus stop; arriving by car – Burgh Castle car park)

Parking NR31 9QG
Burgh Castle car park, Butt Lane

Public toilets
None (Queen's Head for customers)

Cafés/pubs
Queen's Head

Terrain
Pavement and lanes; grassy and crushed-stone paths; boardwalk

Hilliness
Level throughout

Did you know? Many centuries after the last Roman soldier had abandoned Britannia, the Normans breathed new life into Burgh Castle. Using its high walls as a ready-made bailey, they threw up a high mound in the south-west corner to create a motte-and-bailey castle. The motte was flattened over a century ago but you can still see where the latter-day invaders dug a large ditch through the south wall.

Local legend In the 13th century, an exiled German named Baron Rudolph Scarfe came to live at Burgh Castle. His reputation for wickedness soon became known far and wide and it was a relief to the locals when he was eventually killed. However, the Devil transformed him into a hound of hell with black fur and bright red eyes and sent him back to Earth. Old Scarfe was still causing havoc centuries later.

Footwear
Winter
Spring/Summer/Autumn

Public transport
Bus service 5 between Great Yarmouth, Bradwell and Burgh Castle (bus stop at ❼): firstbus.co.uk/norfolk-suffolk

Accessibility
Suitable for powered wheelchairs and all-terrain pushchairs, except for the spur ❼ to ❾ and allowing for a grassy path between ❺ and ❻

Dogs
Welcome, but keep on leads at Burgh Castle Roman fort. No stiles

Walk 10 Burgh Castle

STORIES BEHIND THE WALK

St Peter and St Paul's Church Hidden in its own little copse, it's easy to miss this ancient church, even though the walk passes it twice. Its round tower and parts of the nave date back to late Saxon times, while the remainder is medieval. Look out for the Roman tiles in the walls, no doubt filched from the abandoned fort next door. If you want to look inside, the church is open daily from 10am–5pm from April to October and 10am–3.30pm in November.

Breydon Water Most of the Norfolk Broads were created by the flooding of medieval peat workings – a discovery made by botanist Dr Joyce Lambert as recently as the 1950s. However, Breydon Water is a remnant of what was once called the Great Estuary, which flowed straight out to sea to the east. Today, with the picturesque rivers Yare and Waveney at its western end, Breydon Water's 1,200 acres form part of an RSPB nature reserve.

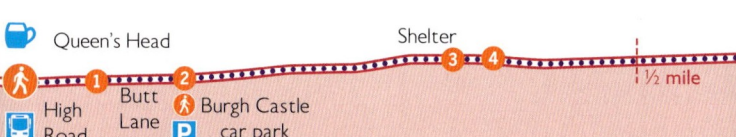

Start – arriving by bus
➡ With the Queen's Head pub to your right, walk along the road towards the village to the first turning on the left.

1 ➡ Go **left** along Butt Lane for 150 yards to the brown Burgh Castle sign.

76 Short Walks Made Easy